This Is My Story, This Is My Song

(I Never Walked Alone)

WILMA L MCGEE

This Is My Story, This Is My Song
(I Never Walked Alone)

WILMA L MCGEE

905 S. Douglas Ave. • Nashville, Tennessee 37204
615-972-2842
Lowbarpublishingcompany@gmail.com
www.Lowbarbookstore.com

Printed in the United States of America
LOWBAR PUBLISHING COMPANY

ISBN: 978-0-9862771-5-3
905 S. Douglas Ave.
Nashville, Tennessee 37204
615-972-2842
Lowbarpublishingcompany@gmail.com
www.Lowbarbookstore.com

For additional information and details on workshops and seminars, please contact the author:
Wilma L. McGee
P.O. Box 456
Hazel Park, Michigan 48030-0456
313-770-0458
babydoll1948@sbcglobal.net

Editor: Jody Amato
Graphic and cover design artist: Norah S. Branch
Layout Artist: Vashon Oggs

No part of this book may be reproduced or transmitted in any form or by any means, graphic, electronic, or mechanical, including photocopying, recording, taping, or by any information storage retrieval system, without the permission, in writing, of the publisher or author.

Scripture references in this book are taken from the King James Version (KJV) of the *Holy Bible* unless otherwise noted.
Printed in the United States of America

Copyright © 2015 Wilma L. McGee

CONTENTS

Foreword	*7*
Introduction	*8*
Chapter 1 In the Beginning	*13*
Chapter 2 Blessed Be the Ties that Bind	*20*
Chapter 3 I Remember Daddy	*31*
Chapter 4 Make Me Over, Lord, Extremely	*37*
Chapter 5 This Is My Story, This Is My Song Part I	*45*
Chapter 6 This Is My Story, This Is My Song Part II	*53*
Chapter 7 This Is My Story, This Is My Song Part III	*60*
Chapter 8 Many Things about Tomorrow	*64*
Chapter 9 Whether I Live or Die, I Win!	*69*

FOREWORD

This is the story of my wife's journey (Wilma McGee), the songs she would sing and the scriptures she read that would be of help to her as she went through the challenges she faced. She would often go to the scriptures, such as Isaiah 54:17 *No weapon that is formed against thee shall prosper; and every tongue that shall rise against thee in judgment thou shalt condemn. This is the heritage of the servants of the Lord, and their righteousness is of me, saith the Lord.* After reading the scripture, she would pray, sing, and sit back and watch God work. He tells us in His word to be patient, to believe and to trust in Him.

I found out that He always worked things out. Through sickness, He was there. Through the good times, he was there. We know now that we were and are never alone.

I thank God first and then my wife for doing such a wonderful job in writing this book. Through our experiences together, we are still leaning and depending on Jesus Christ because He said, "I will never leave you nor forsake you."

It is my prayer that the reader will be blessed and gain a sense of security through reading God's Word, begin a relationship with Him, and learn to lean and depend upon Him.

Respectfully submitted,
Rev. Herman McGee
Assistant to the Pastor
Sweet Kingdom Missionary Baptist Church
(Rev. Robert B. Jones Sr., Pastor)
4150 Chene
Detroit, Michigan 48207

INTRODUCTION

How does one handle the ups and downs of life? Life's big surprises—like when suddenly, from out of nowhere, your job is no longer your job. Should you be frightened, or is this another one of God's promotions? As your employer smugly tells you that your services are no longer needed, they seem to have forgotten that you didn't even apply for the position, but were called for it. They don't know that "your" Father in Heaven works as in **Philippians 4:19** *But my God shall* **supply all your need** *according to His riches in glory by Christ Jesus.*

What do you do when you find yourself in an abusive relationship and the other party decides if he can't have you no one will and instead of just leaving, he decides to try to end your life. You feel the threat of life being taken from you, leaving you . . . and you remember those you love and you begin to fight back. You prevail to live, yet are filled with fear. You remember **Psalm 23:4** *Yea, though I walk through the valley of the shadow of death . . .*

What do you do when one of those closest to you, one of those beloved that you just fought to live for, is stricken with an incurable sickness. The doctor does what he can, but God calls that person home by name and you are left behind.

What do you do when you trusted someone enough to go out with for the first time, and he refuses to accept that "no means no!"

What do you do when that spouse you married, thinking he or she was surely sent from heaven, but turns out to be from that other place!

What do you do when you or your child are robbed by an armed perpetrator who says, "Don't make this no murder," or "Give me that jacket and those shoes."

Or when you're still living and making plans and suddenly are given a serious or even terminal diagnosis.

Wow! What do you do? Do you sing, "This is my story, this is my song, praising my Savior, all the day long"?

This book recounts a journey of length, some sixty-six-plus years. It starts in the beginning and fast forwards to the days when I learned about God, when I knew about Him, eventually came to know Him for myself and share, "Look where He brought me from!" It is a journey of the challenges I faced along the way and how God, even when I didn't know Him and possibly even *chose* not to know Him, as we sometimes do, brought me through.

As I journeyed through this life and came to know Him for myself, "I never walked alone." These pages come from my heart, scanning through the years of growing up, being on my own, and searching for something, I didn't know what, who, or where. I was told I was looking for love in all the wrong places. What a true statement: for I learned that *for God is love* (**1 John 4:8b**). Love was so near, yet so far, because of my lack of knowledge.

When challenges appear in our lives, some of us cry, others become angry and may take that anger out on others (mostly those we are closest to). We burn bridges that we may need to cross over again. Some of us just walk away or go into hiding, hoping it will all go away. Some say, "I can't take this anymore!" and make a sad attempt to end it all.

What do *you* do? Some read the Word of God, some choose to pray, some choose to sing songs, as is written in **Ephesians 5:19** *Speaking to yourselves in psalms and hymns and spiritual songs, singing and making melody in your heart to the Lord.* **James 5:13** *Is any among you afflicted? Let him pray. Is any merry? Let him sing psalms.* I have learned to do both: pray and sing psalms/songs. I remember as a child how my mother would kiss the hurt, hum a medley of songs, and my tears would stop. Or when I was sleepy, she would take me in her arms and sing to me as I fell asleep. I have learned what a blessing is in singing the Lord's songs!

Psalm 137:4 *How shall we sing the Lord's song in a strange land?* What is the strange land that you may be in right now? Would it be where you live, your state of mind, or just a change in your plans as you're faced with something unexpected? Are you in a strange land and unable to sing the Lord's songs? Sing! Sing! Sing!

This is truly my story of the peace that passes all understanding, even in what would seem cumbersome situations. One instance in particular is my story of planning what my next step would be as I approached retirement age, sixty-two, in 2010. These words are found in **Jeremiah 29:11** *For I know the thoughts that I think toward you, saith the Lord, thoughts of peace, and not of evil, to give you an expected end.* (From the **New International Version**) *"For I know the plans I have for you," declares the Lord, "plans to prosper you and not to harm you, plans to give you hope and a future."*

My plans included more time for travel with my husband, my "BabyDoll"; continuing to work part time in a nursing capacity with medically fragile children; attending different events, especially Christian education conferences; and having more time and freedom to be my husband's helpmeet in ministry, available to continue what we were really already doing. This is my story of the scriptures I read, or that the Lord would bring to my mind, and songs I would sing or hum when I couldn't find the words to say in prayer or in general when I was in "my strange land."

"This is my story, this is my song, praising my Savior, all the day long" is to encourage you to do the same. Praise God in all that you go through. My prayer is that you, the reader, will assuredly want to acquire more faith and trust in God, that you will come to realize that He is truly in control of everything and everybody—the good, the bad, or the indifferent. You will come to know the peace that passes all understanding. I know I did!

After my first writing, *Heeeeeeeeey!!! I'm Just A "Sista" Tryin' To Tell Somebody About Jesus*, I was asked frequently if I was giving my testimony. I would always say, "No, not yet! That will come later." And here it is. I always say this is "our book," meaning God and me, because He gave me the inspiration to write for Him and about Him.

When I began that first book in 2009, I had no idea that I would even have a testimony to tell, not realizing that every day God allows me to open my eyes, be in my right mind, breathe His air, and have the use of all my limbs was, in fact, a testimony. I am now telling everyone who will listen what Jesus, whom I was talking about in book one, has done for me, thinking that one needs to know about Him first in order to understand His power.

So many times when things happen that are not according to our plans, we become angry (**Ephesians 4:26** *Be ye angry, and sin not: let not the sun go down upon your wrath*) and resentful; nothing is what we intended it to be. We have a tendency to want to give up and throw in the towel. Perhaps we think that life is supposed to be a big bowl of cherries (if that is what we like), but then life tosses us a lemon and we pucker because it is sour when we could just add the "sweetness of Jesus" and make some lemonade! We can have as much of Him as we want and He will only do us good, because He came: **John 10:10b** . . . *I am come that they might have life, and that they might have it more abundantly.*

What we must realize is that life is a period of time in humanity, beginning at our birth until God calls our name and we answer from death into Life. *Man that is born of a woman is of few days, and full of trouble* (**Job 14:1**). Is this perhaps because of sin, the sin that began in the Garden of Eden? Think on these things. What is important is how we handle the challenges and the blessings that come during that period of time we call life. Things will happen, some good and some not so good, but we must keep our focus on God and the fact that it is He who has made us and not we ourselves. He is in control.

I give testimony of the God whom I serve, praise, and worship. Again, I encourage those who are going through difficult situations that, even though things may seem impossible, with God all is possible. We need to realize that God knows all there is to know about us and it is not taking Him by surprise! He knows everything that is, has been, and is to come, and my desire is to help prepare others for the trials and tests that will come in life. My purpose is to shed more light on the *Light*.

Blessed assurance, Jesus, (The Light) is mine,
This is my story, this is my song, praising my Savior, all the day long.

CHAPTER 1

IN THE BEGINNING
O LITTLE TOWN OF PORT HURON

To tell my story, I must start at the beginning.

Once upon a time, in the little town of Port Huron, Michigan, on a hot summer day—June 24, 1948, to be exact—a bouncing baby girl was born to a wonderful couple, King and Wilma Thomason. My mother always told me that they were going to keep trying until they had a little girl and that girl would be me, yours truly. I came as a shock to all! There were no ultrasounds or tests to determine gender back then, so there was no advance knowledge of the sex of the child. You would only find out upon arrival and I arrived as a princess into a family with four "princes." Nevertheless, there was a change in their lives! A girl among four boys: King III, Henry, Walter, Bernard, and finally Wilma (Billie). None followed me. (I once created a black history presentation during which, when introducing myself, I said that I came from royalty. "My grandfather's name was King, my father's name was King, I have a brother named King, and I hail from 'The King.' That is true royalty!").

In the days of my childhood, I learned the importance of family togetherness. For example, we always ate dinner together. It didn't matter what time, we waited for my father to come in from work and then we would all sit down. Grace was said and we each recited a verse from the Bible before we ate. Whatever happened to those days? As a single mom, I did teach that to my son, but as time went on, with my working, his schooling and eventually having a job, we let that time get away from us, sitting down and saying the blessing and eating together. Now there are TV tables and you eat when "you" are ready.

That training was such a vital part in my upbringing. There were no cell phones and at one time we didn't have a TV, only the radio. Radios? What are those? Dinner was kind of a family quiet time because "you didn't talk with food in your mouth!" When there was talk it was usually between my mother and father, and the children didn't speak unless spoken too! Shortly after dinner it was bedtime and "now I lay me down to sleep" every night without fail.

As I look back over my life, I have a testimony. We went to church three to four times on Sunday: Sunday school, morning service, 3:00 p.m. service, BTU, and 7:00 p.m. service. Mom was the church organist and pianist for years. My father was chairman of the Deacon Board, I believe before I was even born, and served until he was eighty-five years of age. He became a mentor, training the younger men, preparing and encouraging them to step up as he stepped down. I think about Dad's actions: as he realized he was getting on in years and would not be able to perform the tasks of the chairman of the deacons, he chose to move over and adhere to the teachings of **Titus 2,** in which instructions are given to the men and women to teach the younger men and women. (Food for thought: I know that carrying a title gives status and with status comes perks, right? However, it is good to pass the torch so that the works of the Lord may continue. When we become stagnant in our ministry and the people are not growing, we should remove ourselves from our position, seek God's guidance, and become mentors to those who come after. Perhaps God has taken you as far as He wants you to go in that particular ministry and is positioning you for His next mission for you.)

I guess one could say that I was a "CDK" (chairman of the deacons' kid), like a "PK" (preacher's kid). My parents truly believed in **Proverbs 22:6** *Train up a child in the way he should go: and when he is old, he will not depart from it.* I once turned away from the faith, but only briefly because of this particular scripture, along with the prayers and teachings of my mother and father.

Unlike some, I was blessed to live in a house with both parents present, from the time I was born until adulthood. When taught by "born-again" parents, it isn't so much that they sit down and say, "Do this," and "Don't do that," but rather that they teach by the way they live. And in this way they instill a tendency to "remember your upbringing," making it difficult to turn away completely and permanently. We were a family that believed in family values and were taught when going out on our own with friends, we should "remember our name!" I always tie that in when it comes to my walk with the Lord. I have to remember "whose" I am. My name in Christ as in **Titus 2:7-8** *In all things shewing thyself a pattern of good works: in doctrine shewing uncorruptness, gravity, sincerity, sound speech, that cannot be condemned; that he that is of the contrary part may be ashamed, having no evil thing to say of you.* In other words, I need to carry myself as if I am representing Christ at all times. It was the same in my home, so that there would be no talk against the family name. My parents took pride in our name, and friends and neighbors knew that there was a certain characteristic about our family members that we maintained, so as not to bring shame to our name. That was not just in my immediate family, but the entire extended family. My father had seven brothers and four sisters and his father was a minister, so there wasn't much room for deviation. Mind you now, we were far from being *sinless*, but we strived to *sin less*. Just as we have access to the Father by Christ Jesus, so did people in the community have access to our father by way of the telephone if they saw us doing anything wrong. They sought out our father here on earth!

I did make the decision to try another faith; however, they were teaching against Christ, saying He was not born of a virgin, their philosophy being, "You know what you did to have your son." I thought, *They can't possibly be serious!* To me that was blasphemy, something that truly was against what I had learned in

Sunday school and church. It was truly contrary, especially when they told you whom to believe in, but didn't have the sound doctrine of the Word to support their theory. That sent up a red flag: stop! My first thought was that my parents would not have taught me a lie. I refer to my parents first because they were my first teachers and, though I was being taught about Christ, my faith was in them because I knew them. I didn't know Christ, I didn't know the Bible, but I was learning. I had that child-like faith in Mom and Dad, which stayed with me until I came to know the Lord for myself and I came to have faith in God. I remembered reading that with God all things were possible and that stayed with me, even as I accepted the Lord into my life years later and came into the understanding of that same scripture, believing even more so.

Growing up, my first love was singing, and I had my first solo at the age of five, singing "All Night, All Day, Angels Watching over Me." My pastor at the time (now deceased) always wanted me to sing that song. On any given Sunday he would say, "I want my 'baby' to come and sing for me" and I would hop right up out of my seat, so proud, and start singing. As I got older, I didn't want to sing that song anymore—it was for babies! The older I got, the more I resented it; he would still say, "I want my 'baby' to come and sing for me" when I was seventeen! Really? Who does that? Well, some forty-five-plus years later, I am still singing "All night, all day, the angels keep watching over me." I have found it to be true and I thank God for His angels watching over me!

I think of my mother as the musician then, and how she would always say, "Sing it like you mean it." At five I was being "the cute little girl singing." At seventeen, I was the "rebellious teen." I didn't want to sing, didn't want to go to church, didn't know God, and probably didn't want to know Him. I only knew about Him, and there is a difference between knowing about Him and knowing Him for oneself. I thought, *When I get big, I ain't going to no church and I ain't going to do my kids like my parents did us.*" Ha! Ha! Ha! "He who laughs last, laughs first!" I imagine God laughed at me back then! Thank God for His Word, and oh, how true is **Proverbs 22:6** *Train up a child in the way he should go: and when he is old, he will not depart from it.*

Down through the years, God has been good to me. The angels were and are still watching over me. **Psalm 91:11** *For He shall give His angels charge over thee, to keep thee in all thy ways.*

Beyond rebellion, some years later I experienced what I call a "Job moment," in that I had a skin problem all over my body, except for my face. When going through that challenge, I thought of Job, when Satan was allowed to inflict him with boils all over his body. I wondered if God said, "Have you considered my servant, Wilma?" It was during that time that Job's wife came to him and asked: *Then said his wife unto him, dost thou still retain thine integrity? Curse God, and die. But he said unto her, Thou speakest as one of the foolish women speaketh. What? Shall we receive good at the hand of God, and shall we not receive evil? In all this did not Job sin with his lips.* (**Job 2:9-10**) It is said of Job in scripture; *there was a man in the land of Uz, whose name was Job;* **and that man was perfect and upright, and one that feared God, and eschewed evil** (**Job 1:1**).

The phrase "the patience of Job" is often mentioned when one is going through a trial or test. Just what is the patience of Job? What is patience? Patience is the quality of being patient, as in the bearing of provocation, annoyance, misfortune, or pain, without complaint, loss of temper, irritation, or the like. We learn that Job loses his children, his livestock, and his body is inflicted with boils. In the story he was distraught, and *he did complain,* as any human would, but he never cursed God. He always offered prayer and sacrifice for the sins that may have occurred during family gatherings and celebrations; he always gave reverence to God. As noted previously, **Job 2:10b** *In all this did not Job sin with his lips.*

It seems in reading and studying Job that he was fine with God in all that he was going through; even when his wife tried to entice him to curse God and die, he remained steadfast. Then his friends came to visit and that's when things changed. He seemed to become bitter. He lost his focus on God and started listening to his friends, but he never sinned with his lips against God.

When someone we love is going through a difficult or painful time, we have a tendency to offer pity or our opinions, as was the case with Job and his friends. We want to know the reason for everything, because there must be something we aren't doing right, right? Sometimes it is best to practice **Psalm 46:10a** *Be still, and know that I am God.* It is best to just be quiet and listen to the person who is going through the "wilderness" or is in that "strange land."

Why is it when trials and tests come upon us, the first thing we do is try to determine the reason? Perhaps our thoughts should be, "Okay, God, I am listening, you have my attention." Perhaps it is just human nature, but we have a pity party instead of a praise party. We want everyone who will agree with the negative to keep it going. Okay, so how are you going to have a praise party when you've lost your children, your job becomes obsolete, your spouse is "speaking as one of the foolish women," you are facing health challenges, or loved ones are dying when you least expect it? What is your "strange land" experience? What do you do? *Wherefore take unto you the whole armour of God, that ye may be able to withstand in the evil day, and having done all, to stand* (**Ephesians 6:13**). Be as Christ when in the wilderness and say, "Get thee behind me, Satan!"

Think of Job's situation again: **Job 1:1** *. . . and that man was perfect and upright, and one that feared God, and eschewed evil.* In the midst of it all, there was a blessing for Job. In the midst of all that you may be going through, there is a blessing for you. There is the belief that once we accept Jesus as our Lord and Savior, everything is going to be wonderful; but God did not, nor does He promise to, make our lives "smooth sailing" always. Jesus is speaking here: *These things I have spoken unto you, that in me ye might have peace. In the world ye shall have tribulation: but be of good cheer; I have overcome the world* (**John 16:33**). Also, from **Romans 8:28** *And* *we know that all things work together for good to them that love God, to them who are the called according to **His** purpose.* Jesus has overcome the world for us and He has "***His***" purpose for our lives. Be of good cheer.

The skin issue came about when I was in my late twenties, a divorced and single mother living in Detroit, Michigan. I didn't know God, but as I stated previously, I knew about Him; I thought of Job's condition at that time and thought, *I am going to handle this like he did.* I again wondered if God had asked Satan, "Have you considered my servant, Wilma"? People would look at me and back away. I was a nurse and worked in a hospital; can you imagine your nurse coming in with flakey skin and bumps from head to toe? I had patients to care for and they were looking at me strangely, as if to say, "Is that contagious? Should you be here, and with me?" At church I stopped extending my hands in fellowship because, yes, my Christian brothers and sisters would hesitate. You know the handshake that is not a handshake, but a mere brushing and not touching? Greeting each other with a "holy kiss?" That was not happening, and believe me, I understood. I was under the care of a dermatologist, but my skin condition was still the "unknown" to them, something not to touch for fear of what could happen.

My spirits were tumbling down and my self-esteem was at rock bottom. I praise God for my friends; one in particular, if she is reading this, I am sure remembers this incident. She was a true friend, indeed. She suggested, "Let's go to the park and take the kids and get in the water." I thought, *You must be crazy! Look at me! I look horrible!* But I agreed. I prepared to get in the water, but I kept my jeans and a light jacket on over my swimsuit because I didn't want anyone staring at me. My friend snatched my jacket away, drawing attention from the people around. The comments I heard were, "Wow! Look at them freckles!" I thought they must have poor eyesight, but it made me think the scars could pass for freckles. I smiled. I chuckled. I even laughed. I began to have fun again.

Oh, how I love Jesus, because He first loved me.

CHAPTER 2

BLESSED BE THE TIES THAT BIND WOMEN IN MY LIFE

The aged women likewise, that they be in behaviour as becometh holiness, not false accusers, not given to much wine, teachers of good things; that they may teach the young women to be sober, to love their husbands, to love their children, to be discreet, chaste, keepers at home, good, obedient to their own husbands, that the word of God be not blasphemed. **Titus 2:3-5**

When you think of the women in your life, which person comes to mind? Mama! She would probably be number one; after all, she gave birth to you. She was the vessel God chose in giving you life. She nurtured you from the time you were conceived within the womb. She fed you. You were kept warm within and life flowed through your body just as it did hers. You were there, in most cases, for nine months. She waited on you to mature enough to face life. On the day you were born, the day you separated yourself from the womb (after all, you had to make your debut into society), your first love affair began. It was love at first sight! Mama! What a woman!

It was not a one-sided affair, for any mother falls in love with that newborn baby who fought his or her way while in the womb to develop into the life that is now thought to be so helpless; yet even on that day, you came into being in charge and full of trouble.

Job 14:1 *Man that is born of a woman is of few days, and full of trouble.*

Though there were many women in my life, my mother and grandmother were the main two whose presence I grew up in. They were just as the scripture describes "teachers of good things." They were different in personality, but they had Christ in common. They contributed much to my growth into womanhood and into the Christian woman I am today. They were my role models, my examples of virtuous women. They were also of the group in **James 5:16b** *The effectual fervent prayer of a righteous man availeth much.* They prayed for me!

Mama. I remember my mother.

That woman who gave birth to me, named me after her, fed me my first meal; she was the woman who taught me my first song and my first prayer. Though she was a very serious person most of the time, she showed us a comical side, too. Her laughter was the kind that drew attention from those who heard her and it caused them to laugh as well. I never saw her cry; but I knew when she was disturbed, especially if someone was bothering her children. You didn't want to see that side. Because she was such a mild-mannered person, you would not like her when she was angry. She was stern in disciplinary actions—she said what she meant and meant what she said, and you had better know it!

In my adolescent years, I guess I was pretty "mouthy"—actually there is no guessing, I was! Mama wouldn't say anything; she never threatened me or said, "Wait until your dad gets home," and never made empty promises. Today when we tell our children, "Do it one more time and I am going to . . ." sometimes they do it four or five more times and we never follow through. Mama followed through when and where it happened and if that meant a "back-handed lick to the mouth," I got it! I often said that I remember the back of her hand as if I had just seen it yesterday, because it seemed that I was always saying something I shouldn't! I could see her hand coming, but I never was able to move fast enough for her to miss. That probably would not have been a good idea anyway. Things probably would have been much worse. Oh, how I remember Mama!

Back then, mothers could also read our minds somehow. I don't quite remember the issue, but once we weren't on the same page about something. I got an attitude and I murmured under my breath, you know how we do when things aren't going the way we think they should, "You make me sick!" I don't know what it was, but she couldn't have heard me, it was just in my mind! She said, "Oh! So I make you sick? Well let me show you just how sick I can make you!" Whatever was in her hand had me ducking and dodging for what seemed like hours. Child abuse laws had not come into play then and when I think back to those days and the fact that children learn what they hear, see, and "feel," I am grateful for my upbringing, even though I might not have been at the time. I often said that I was adopted because I was always seeing the back of my mother's hand and I didn't get to have things my way. After all, I felt since I was the "princess," the only girl, I should get everything I wanted. Not! Instead, I got everything I needed. Praise God!

My mother was truly a strong Christian woman, as I came to learn. It was funny, because I just knew that she wasn't saved. I thought, *She ain't saved 'cause she don't even get happy and shout!* But her strength was amazing. (This is evidence that what one doesn't see in another doesn't make them any more or less saved than the next individual.) Her faith and trust in God were not based on what I saw, and it became evident to me by her actions . . . her walk and her talk . . . especially when she became ill. I thought that if anything serious ever came my way, I would want to be as strong in my faith as she was in hers. I wonder sometimes if that was a request that I didn't realize at the time I was making, as God allowed tests of my faith and trust in Him to come later in my life. I have heard it said, "Be careful what you ask God for, He may just grant it—and not according to what you imagined." I remember an aunt asking my mother, while she was in the hospital, if she was afraid. She said, "No, because I have faith in God and if I have faith, I don't have to be afraid." Her favorite song was "I Know Who Holds Tomorrow" (it has become mine through the years). She never seemed to worry about anything. I often heard her say, "We just have to trust in the Lord," and she did. Her days began with prayer, reading and studying her Bible, and riding her stationary bike. She was up every morning by five, spending time with God. I, too, am learning the practice of spending time with God (I haven't been too faithful with the stationary bike, though). It is truly a blessing and a wonderful way to start your day.

Mama made sure we went to church and Sunday school, put God first, and got a good education; she was insistent that we earn good grades. I graduated from high school in June 1966 and started college in September, entering the School of Practical Nursing in January 1967. In the beginning, nursing wasn't for me, or so I thought. I had to clean a patient during the clinical part of my training, and I didn't want any part of it! Little did I know that nursing was more than what I saw at age six when I had my tonsils out: nurses did more than wear a white dress, a cute cap, and carry a little tray with pills on it. I went home from school that day and told my mother, "I don't want to be a nurse anymore." I wanted to throw in the towel. Bedpans? Cleaning dentures? Feeding people that weren't babies, are you *serious*? Somehow she persuaded me to hang in there, so I kept going, and soon discovered it wasn't just a job to me, but a ministry to the sick, whether mental, physical, emotional, or spiritual. It turned out to be something that I truly love doing: helping people to get well and to also be well.

Mama was my greatest supporter in everything I did: singing, baking, or whatever I was attempting, she was there for me. She was also a believer in experience is the best teacher. At fifteen, I decided I was going to learn how to smoke to keep up with the other girls my age. What a lesson! She and my father were both away from home, probably working. I was home alone and thought that this was my chance to practice smoking so I could fit in.

How quickly I learned that experience is the best teacher, which my mother so fondly believed. I took a puff on a cigarette and opened the kitchen window so I could blow the smoke out; but just as I did a gust of wind came through the window, blew the smoke back in my face and I began to choke. When I looked out the other window and saw Mom coming up the street, I panicked and started choking even more. I was choking until the Jesus that I "thought I only knew about" came to mind and I said "Lord, if you just let me live this time, I will never smoke again." Praise God for my mother. It seemed that when she saw me she knew what I had been up to and never said a word. She may have thought I had been punished enough already. To this day, I am not a smoker and I never have been!

The lessons of life—the "girl talk"—I missed coming from my mother. She was raised by her grandmother, because her mother passed when she was six years old. At eighteen, her grandmother passed, and I guess she never had those conversations so vital to girls and young ladies growing up, the facts of life. On different occasions I tried to ask questions, and I remember asking her about birth control after I married. Her reply was, "How dare you ask me such a question!" But she thought about it and came back to me later that day to talk about birth control, and that began the first of many open discussions. You see, she came from an era in which such talk was disrespectful for both the person asking the question and the person being asked. Nice girls didn't talk about stuff like that. She always thought we were taught the facts of life in school, in home economics and gym class. It never occurred to her that I wouldn't know. What I had learned came from reading *True Love* and *True Confessions* magazines and from my girlfriends, who thought they knew everything.

FYI moment here: *The aged women likewise, that they be in behaviour as becometh holiness, not false accusers, not given to much wine, teachers of good things; that they may teach the young women . . .* (**Titus 2:3-4a**). It seems that in today's society anything and everything goes. Scripture is being fulfilled in every moment that we live, move, and have our being. I see young ladies every day carrying themselves in such ways that I would have never dreamed of when I was growing up. I hear in their speech a cry for help, but we aren't listening to them. I remember a gentleman saying once, "You heard me, but you weren't listening." You hear someone talking, but you are not tuned in. They do not have your attention, so you can hear them, but you are not listening to what is being said; you are not focused. The aged women and men—guilty! We have **not** taught: **Titus 2:12** *Teaching us that, denying ungodliness and worldly lusts, we should live soberly, righteously, and godly, in this present world.* Ladies, we need to be teaching our daughters "our Father's business," how to become young women of God. Whatever happened to our being obedient to God's word in teaching our children? As in **Proverbs 9:10** *The fear of the Lord is the beginning of wisdom: and the knowledge of the holy is understanding.*

In "our" first writing, *HEEEEEEEEEY, I'm Just A "Sista" Tryin' To Tell Somebody About Jesus*, the following scripture is referenced several times and is just as important here. **Hosea 4:6** *My people are destroyed for lack of knowledge: because thou hast rejected knowledge, I will also reject thee, that thou shalt be no priest to me: seeing thou hast forgotten the law of thy God, I will also forget thy children.* Ladies, we need to teach our daughters the facts of life according to the Word of God. Not what man says, but what God says. It *is* in His Book!!! The older men should step up and teach the young men how to present themselves before God in order to be the men that God has called them to be.

I could understand my mother's dilemma when it came to talking to me. I was, after all, her first and only daughter. She was raised in an environment where the facts of life were not taught; you learned them on your own or through other girls' conversations. And of course hearing from the "unlearned" or "untaught," things can get somewhat twisted. I believe she had a feeling of embarrassment when it came to that subject because if she could find it in a book, that is how she would pass the information on to me.

Mom was always one for reading labels on canned goods or anything she was going to consume or give to her family. She wasn't going to give us anything she thought would be harmful. She never smoked or consumed alcohol, and I never, ever heard a curse word come from her mouth; that is why I never understood how she was diagnosed with oral cancer in 1979. She had been bothered with a canker sore on the roof of her mouth for some months. (FYI: whenever you have a sore anywhere that does not heal, have it checked as soon as possible to avoid further health problems.) She wouldn't complain; she just dealt with it. I noticed her holding her face one day in discomfort and asked what was wrong, and she told me about the sore. At that time I was a nurse on the oncology unit at the hospital where I worked. I looked at it and it looked very suspicious, so I told one of the doctors about it. He asked to have her to come in to be seen. I suspected it was cancer, but I didn't want to accept that, nor did I say anything to that effect; but after biopsies were done, my suspicions were confirmed and eventually it spread to her brain.

I guess she was trying to prepare me in all of this, as was God, but again, I didn't know Him then. I still only knew *about* Him, but I was making strides to get to know Him. Mom started telling me to look after my father and my youngest brother, who had some challenges. I thought, *what about me?*

I'm the baby of the family! Each time I visited her she would tell me, "Take care of your dad and your brother." Many told me that when I asked, "What about me?" she didn't mention me because she knew that I would be alright.

I had recently joined a new church, was singing in the choir, going to Bible class and Sunday school. When you are a Christian, many have these thoughts in mind: these things don't happen, life is always grand, no worries, no heartaches, no pain. So why was this happening to my mother? Why was this happening to me? *I'm a good person; she is a good person. I try to live a good life and try to treat everybody right, so why my mother?* I thought.

Let's take a look at Christ here, because He was a good person and He treated everybody right, but look what He went through and for what? Us! **2 Corinthians 5:21** *For He hath made Him to be sin for us, who knew no sin; that we might be made the righteousness of God in Him.* Christ did no wrong, but look what happened to Him for our sakes. He was made sin . . . that was not good for Him, but it was good for us, for He gave His life for us. Nevertheless, God called my mother's name and she answered on December 22, 1980. I was thirty-two years old. My mother had been the person for me to talk to, my best friend, the one to have lunch with and go shopping with. Mama was the one encouraging me with my son, my nursing career, church, my coming to know the Lord. What was I going to do now? I became angry with her for leaving me. She had no right to do that! I asked her, "Why did you have to leave me? How dare you!" I would go to her gravesite regularly, asking that same question. I never got an answer and I didn't ask God. I dared not ask Him! I didn't know Him and was always taught that you don't question God, and so I didn't. *Be not dismayed, what 'ere be tide, God will take care of you.*

"Gran-maw," as we called her, the second most important woman in my life, was my paternal grandmother. She was there all the time, it seemed. She was our babysitter when our parents would go on vacation and that was always so much fun! It reminds me of the saying printed on babies' t-shirts, "If mama says no, ask grandma." That is how it was when she came to stay with us. I had a tough time losing Mama, but God had gotten me through. My grandmother's prayers helped me get through. When you lose someone to death, you never get over it, but God will get you through it.

My grandmother was always just a phone call away and I started to depend on her for wisdom and knowledge about God. She was very instrumental in my walk with the Lord. If I was having a problem, I could call her any time and she would pray over the phone with me. I remember when growing up, on the first Sunday of the month I was one of the "altar girls" for communion. The altar girls were split into two groups and would sit at each end of the communion table. One group would recite eight verses of scripture before communion and the other group would recite scripture afterward. We wore white, just like the deaconesses did. This particular Sunday, my white skirt was a bit short. Out of the corner of my eye, I saw my grandmother trying to get my attention to cover my lap because of my short skirt, but I chose to ignore her. We didn't have lap hankies then, so she brought a sheet up and draped my lap with it. I couldn't believe she did that and my mother was sitting with the deaconesses, cracking up with laughter.

I was embarrassed beyond embarrassment. But I loved my grandmother, even with that. I was mad, but I got over it fast, before church was out, because I knew there would be consequences to pay if I didn't. Gran-maw was there to encourage me after Mom passed and was a strong Christian woman, a prime example of the "older women teaching the younger women," whether we liked it or not, and believe me, she lived by the Word of God. I often would laugh and think she had lost her mind because I would visit her and she would be in the house singing, shouting, and praising the Lord. One song I remember her singing was "The Lord Is my Shepherd and I Shall Not Want." I thought, *this is not even Sunday, and she ain't even at church!* Perhaps she was in a "strange land" and needed to sing the Lord's song. She was having church! Growing up, that was just c-r-a-z-y to me! Over the years, however, I find myself doing the same. I remember an incident involving her, me, and many of my cousins. Our church was across the street from her house. Every Sunday when church let out we would head straight to gran-maw's house. Now, we knew she definitely did not approve of dancing of any kind, and we had the nerve to dance in her house! How crazy was that? We knew she would be coming home at any moment, but we would still take the chance, put the records on and start dancing (and not holy dancing, either). We would be watching for her so we could turn off the music and sit down before she came in, like we were so innocent. We didn't see her coming this particular Sunday and she came in the house like Jesus did when He was cleaning out the temple, saying, "God don't like ugly and it's a shame fo' God!" Anything she felt that was not of God was ugly and a shame before Him!

I understand her ways now that I have come to know Him for myself and have a relationship with Him. I find myself praising God in my home and some mornings, when on my way to work, I have had to pull over because I was listening to Christian radio and got caught up in the Spirit so that I needed to calm down before I could continue driving. What a mighty God we serve! You cannot come in contact with the Lord and remain the same if you have truly accepted him as your Lord and Savior. **2 Corinthians 5:17** *Therefore if any man be in Christ, he is a new creature: old things are passed away; behold, all things are become new.*

Gran-maw became ill and I thought, *Here we go again.* She was the main tie to our family, the matriarch, "the binding tie." God called her name, and she answered in June 1984. She had often told me that I would miss her when she was gone (oh, how true those words) and as I think now, maybe that was her way of preparing me for her passing. She, too, often said for me to look after my dad after my mother passed and I did just that, along with my brothers.

There were many other women in my life that were like mentors to me: aunts, church mothers, older Christian sisters, older cousins, and mom's best friend. I met many going to the women's conferences on many occasions and through church fellowships. It is so important to follow with what is written in **Hebrews 10:24-25** *And let us consider one another to provoke unto love and to good works: Not forsaking the assembling of ourselves together, as the manner of some is; but exhorting one another: and so much the more, as ye see the day approaching.* They held true to the scripture of being "teachers of good things." They were living testimonies of a life in Christ. They taught me how to act and how not to act and I praise God for them all.

> *Blessed be the tie(s) that binds, our hearts in Christian love;*
> *the fellowship of kindred minds, is like to that above.*

CHAPTER 3

I REMEMBER DADDY

As a small child, who do we cling to when we are overcome by fear of the unknown? In whose arms can we find comfort and into whose lap can we climb for that sense of security? Who is it that in our "toddling" stages seems so tall and strong, and he reaches down to take our hands to hold us up as we take our first steps? Daddy. We cling to him as he clings to God, whose hand he holds.

Proverbs 17:6 *Children's children are the crown of old men; and the glory of children are their fathers.*

As I said, I was brought up in a strict Christian environment. My parents lived according to the word of God and taught us the same: again, not so much to do this or that, but to follow their example before us. There was no card playing, no dice (so no Monopoly games), no drinking, no swearing, no smoking, and certainly, at that age for me, definitely no boys! There was never any back talk with my father; he did not play around! He just had that "look."

"You are going to Sunday school and church as long as you live under this roof. You will abide by my rules and if you don't like it, you can get out!" What? Are you serious? Yes! I thought, *Not me, because I am the princess!* Boy or girl, there were no exceptions to his rules. I felt like Daddy was tough on my brothers, but since I was a daddy's girl, I should be able to get away with anything. No! He was even tougher on me. For instance, I had my first kiss in my daddy's car (what nerve, but scared to death), on LaBelle Street in Highland Park and got busted by my dad! That's when I got the nickname "Wild Bill" by one of my cousins. She still calls me that today!

You had to know my father. I thought for sure *I* was going to die. I had already been told that if I got pregnant and wasn't married, I was going to a home for unwed mothers. Can you imagine that? At age fifteen I had my first kiss; soon after Mother Nature made her first appearance and I started packing my bags to go to a home for unwed mothers because I thought I was pregnant. I thought I would never see my parents again. How horrified I was at that thought! Needless to say, I didn't have to go away. I wasn't pregnant and hadn't done anything to get pregnant, but *I* didn't know that. Being naïve in this instance was probably best for me. Remember, mothers: teach your daughters!

That was a lesson well taught, however, because I became a good fighter, keeping the boys away until I was married. I don't know to this day if I would have ended up in a home for unwed mothers or not. Some say Daddy would not have sent me away, but he made a believer out of me and I wasn't interested in trying to find out. Daddy did not play! When I was in college, I had a movie date with a fellow student. *A nice guy*, I thought, and in the long run he probably was, but I never found out! We went to the movies and afterward he told me we would have to wait in his "friend's" car so that he could take us home, so we did. Well that nice guy asked for a kiss and I said, "No, not on the first date." He tried anyway and whew, Jesus! I really left some marks on him!

He obviously had not heard of the phrase "no means no" back then! I was not going to a home for unwed mothers. I think that was a time Daddy started to relax, because I called him to my rescue, no shame in my game! "Daddy, this boy got fresh with me, can you come and get me?" And he did.

The "friend" called to try to make amends for "the guy," but second chances were not an option at that time. Going to a home for unwed mothers was nothing I was taking a chance on happening to me. That was before I learned that a kiss wouldn't have made me an unwed mother.

Another example of my father's sternness was when I wanted to go to the youth center one Wednesday night. It was the high school students' night, and the center was open from 7:30 p.m. until 10 p.m. I was not allowed to stay until it closed. Around six o'clock I would start asking if I could go, so that Daddy would give me permission to go and have me there by 7:30. One night he asked what was I going down there for and I made the mistake of saying so I could dance! Good answer, but the **wrong** answer! That song by Luther Vandross, "Dance with My Father"— not happening! He told me I wasn't supposed to be dancing! I was thinking, *What? That was the only place I could dance.* At home I bought a rug to put on my bedroom floor. I could listen to records, but Daddy's thing was no dancing, so I danced on the rug, hoping he couldn't hear my feet on the floor. After I told him I went to the center to dance, it took him until 8:30 to give me an answer and by that time it was too late. Wow! It closed at ten and he always picked me up to go home at nine. Needless to say, I didn't get there that evening. Ten o'clock was not a time for a "decent young lady to be coming home," but I was with my father! I didn't tell him that, though. It was just in my thoughts.

My father was the kind of man who walked softly and carried a big stick. Not literally, but meaning that he never screamed or hollered at any of us that I can remember, nor anyone else for that matter. For him to be so quiet, he could really talk and for what seemed like hours at a time. He was the kind of father who could just give you the look (that was probably the "big stick"), and you knew to straighten up and fly right or else. When lecture time came around, I would have preferred "a big stick."

Daddy was good with his hands and worked in television repair, tinkering around the house and working on cars. In fact, he taught me how to change the oil and spark plugs in my car back in the late 70s. I called him and he coached me over the phone.

As chairman of the deacons, he definitely had a walk with the Lord. He was so full of wisdom, and I thought the world of him. He was so knowledgeable. He often read books about cars, TV repair, plumbing . . . he was basically self-taught. He would read and study his Bible late at night before he went to bed. His conversations were so deep that one would never know that he never finished school. He was in the sixth grade when he had to quit school to help at home. When I would go home to visit, we would sit up at times until two o'clock in the morning. We would talk and laugh together and eat ice cream and some of Mama's pound cake. I would talk to him about the Lord, about my son, and how to do this or that. There was nothing I couldn't talk to him about. Most times he would listen, and if I asked him something, he would give an answer. It wasn't always the answer I wanted, but he often said, "If you don't want to hear what I have to say, then don't ask," and that was that!

Boys marry girls "just like the girl that married dear old dad." Girls want to marry guys "just like the guy that married dear old mom." In my search for the man of my dreams, I wanted a man like my daddy: loving, caring, and a good father for my children, a good provider, and a Christian man. I learned the search was not for me to conduct when I came across the scripture **Proverbs 18:22** *Whoso findeth a wife findeth a good thing, and obtaineth favour of the Lord.* I remember when my husband now, my BabyDoll, asked Daddy for my hand in marriage . . . he was not having it! Or so we thought. Daddy was pretty comical back then and did eventually give us his blessings. My brothers, on the other hand, were devious too! One in particular wanted to know, "What are you bringing in exchange for my sister?"

My father had remarried after my mom passed and unfortunately my stepmom, "Mama Ruth," passed some nineteen years later. Daddy came to live with my husband and me, until he passed at the ripe age of ninety-two. My husband was great with my dad and I praise God for him. He was a joy in our home and all of my brothers did their part, along with us, in caring for him. Daddy left us on November 2, 2007. God called his name and he answered, closing his eyes seemingly in rest.

I think about how the "princess" name came about. My father could be very humorous at times, after we were all grown. I was in a concert at my church in 1994 or so, and I asked him to introduce me. He began speaking, telling different stories of my childhood and so on, and then he said, "I introduce to some and present to others, princess, Wilma L. Hunter [at that time]" and the church burst into laughter, as did I! When I got up, I was still laughing so hard, I fell on my way to the stage, tore my stockings and scraped my knee, and had to sing in front of all of those people with a big hole in my stocking and a bloody knee. I said, "What an entrance!" And we all laughed even more. I have referred to myself as a "princess" ever since (remember, **I am** a "King's" kid).

Daddy's favorite song was "Amazing Grace," which he would sing every Sunday during devotion. Another song he loved was "On Christ the Solid Rock I Stand." Daddy had a profound love for God and His Word and it showed in his every action. I could go to him with questions and he was able to give an answer most of the time.

When going through his belongings after his passing, I came across his diary from WWII; what a writing to read. Perhaps that is how I acquired my love for writing—through him and, of course, my Heavenly Father.

On December 7, 1944, Dad wrote, "As far as we went we could see bridges had been blown out, houses blown to bits and airports the same, but way up on the very top of a mountain there stood a big beautiful church, right out in the open; it had not been harmed. As far as we could see, most of the French churches are built on a hill or a mountain and they have been left as they were and of those I had the pleasure of visiting was the Notre Dame De La Grande. It had a few battle scars on it because the Nazis used it as a fort, and to get them out it had to be scarred a little. The Lord has said, 'Upon this rock I will build my church and the gates of hell shall not prevail against it.' That is very true. If you had been here then you'd have seen for yourself." From his writings it was easy to visualize his journey and how he trusted so in the Lord.

Whenever he was on program at church to speak, one of his favorite readings was:

I shall not pass this way again...
"I expect to pass through this world but once.
Any good things, therefore, that I can do or any kindness I can show to any fellow human being let me do it now. Let me not defer nor neglect it,
for I shall not pass this way again."
(Stephen Grellet, 1773-1855, French-born Quaker Minister)

CHAPTER 4

MAKE ME OVER, LORD, EXTREMELY! WEIGHT VS. WAIT

Hebrews 12:1 *Wherefore seeing we also are compassed about with so great a cloud of witnesses, let us lay aside every weight, and the sin which doth so easily beset us, and let us run with patience the race that is set before us.* **II Corinthians 4:17** *For our light affliction, which is but for a moment, worketh for us a far more exceeding and eternal weight of glory.*

God called my mother's and grandmother's names and they answered. No more shopping and lunch dates. Daddy answered the call, too; no more prayers over the phone and late-night chats or fatherly advice. I was left behind again, yet I never walked alone, even though it seemed that way. I was searching for happiness. I went here and I went there, I did this and I did that; but never seemed to be satisfied. I experienced many things during my search, many things that my family would probably never have imagined and those that are gone would probably "turn over in their graves" if they knew.

I think of the places I went to, knowing that I shouldn't be there because God was working in me, and working on me. I had a guilty conscience from being raised by Christian parents, knowing they were praying for me. I remember being in the area of a police raid at an after-hour joint and I was not taken in; **look** at God! I was not handcuffed and put in the paddy wagon; **look** at God! I can remember the days of what we called "bar hopping"; I loved to dance and get attention. I barhopped Wednesday through Saturday and would be sitting in church during Sunday morning service waiting on happy hour. I was doing what pleased me, or what I thought pleased me. I was in search of something or someone that I thought would bring me pleasure. But I still did not have joy! The more bars I hopped, the happier I was not! I went one night and someone asked, "What is a nice girl like you doing in a place like this?" I was so embarrassed. I believe God sent that person to ask me that question. I didn't drink and I didn't smoke. I just loved to dance. I had a date one evening that took me to a "club" (like that made a difference); even he said I looked out of place. What? Was there a mark on my forehead or something to let the world know that I did not belong there, that I belonged to God? Why am I here?

Being single, I was looking for a mate, although I had often heard it said, "You won't find the one you marry in a bar." True! I met my "BabyDoll" in church, even though it was many years later; still, he found me. Hallelujah! **Proverbs 18:22** *Whoso findeth a wife findeth a good thing, and obtaineth favour of the Lord.*

I discovered that I had a "weight" problem: excess baggage and an indirect "wait" problem (God was in wait of me and I couldn't even see him). I was leaping and bounding, hitting the pavement hard because I was so heavy with the weight I was carrying, trying to find peace, joy, and happiness. Once again, I was looking for love in all the wrong places. I was so sick of trying to find those things that only God can give, but I didn't know it at the time. He patiently waited for me.

I am reminded of the man at the pool of Bethesda: **John 5: 2, 4-9** *Now there is at Jerusalem by the sheep market a pool, which is called in the Hebrew tongue Bethesda, having five porches. For an angel went down at a certain season into the pool, and troubled the water: whosoever then first after the troubling of* the water stepped in was made whole of whatsoever disease he had. And a certain man was there, which **had an infirmity thirty and eight years**. *When Jesus saw him lie, and knew that he had been now a long time in that case, He saith unto him, Wilt thou be made whole? The impotent man answered him, Sir, I have no man, when the water is troubled, to put me into the pool: but while I am coming, another steppeth down before me. Jesus saith unto him, Rise, take up thy bed, and walk. And immediately the man was made whole, and took up his bed, and walked: and on the same day was the sabbath.* What was he looking for? What was I looking for, for so many years? I went to church Sunday after Sunday, singing in the choir and sometimes ushering for what seemed like thirty-eight long years. It is funny how we search and the things we do in our searching. We think we know what we need, but we are never finding it. **Matthew 6:33** comes to mind: *But seek ye first the kingdom of God, and His righteousness; and all these things shall be added unto you.* As I would sing, "O, Lord Have Mercy," little did I know that in my singing, I was truly crying out to God. There was always a yearning in the pit of my soul. Things were starting to happen within: my soul was not content and could not be content until I came to know Jesus as my Lord and Savior.

A few years back, I liked to watch the TV program *Extreme Makeover*. I would watch how they would tear one house down and build another in its place. Sometimes they would keep the old shell and rebuild around it. I thought, *that is exactly what I need!* I needed a makeover, extremely, in every area of my life: my spiritual walk, my relationships with the opposite sex, my attitude (and I did have one), my relationships with others in general, my job, my tongue. Rebuild me, Lord, please! From the inside out! Whatever it takes, I surrender all.

My prayers had always been to be a better Christian. You see, I became a "Christian" at the age of twelve so that I could sing in the junior choir at church, but I didn't know that I couldn't join until I was fourteen. That burst my bubble. I was carrying the title of "Christian" over the years, but not in my heart. I was re-baptized at the age of twenty-six, and still no change. The song "Lord I Want to Be a Christian, in My Heart, Lord I Want to Be like Jesus, in My Heart" comes to mind. I wasn't there for God, but He was there for me. I got so sick and tired of carrying that "weight" around; I cried out, "Make me over, Lord, extremely!" Right now, Jesus!

How often when in prayer do we say or hear someone say, "Come on Jesus, right now, Lord"? According to **Genesis 1:27, 31** *So God created man in His own image, in the image of God created he him; male and female created he them. And God saw every thing that He had made, and, behold, it was very good. And the evening and the morning were the sixth day.* Also according to **II Peter 3:8** *But, beloved, be not ignorant of this one thing, that one day is with the Lord as a thousand years, and a thousand years as one day.* God made Adam and Eve in less than a day. God has presented to us that a day in His timing is as a thousand years; notice "in His timing" and the word "as." So now the make-me-over shouldn't take long because it is just taking away here and adding there, right? That "right now, Lord?" In my finite-ness, I was trying to do a condensed version, and you know what happens when man does anything on his own. I wanted to be made over instantly, like instant coffee or Kool-Aid: just add water and sugar to taste, stir, and enjoy the cool, refreshing beverage. Not so in Christ. I was made over in "his image."

There was no repentance or regeneration on my part back then. It was like I didn't even have sense enough to come out of the rain, that rain of sin that was nearly drowning me. As in Ezekiel's prophecy, **Ezekiel 12:2** *Son of man, thou dwellest in the midst of a rebellious house, which have eyes to see, and see not; they have ears to hear, and hear not: for they are a rebellious house.* I was trying to see and hear perhaps, but I was accomplishing neither. It wasn't working for me. I was trying to have my cake and eat it too: hear what I wanted and see what I wanted, but I was in the state of the Laodiceans of **Revelation 3:15-16** *I know thy works, that thou art neither cold nor hot: I would thou wert cold or hot. So then because thou art lukewarm, and neither cold nor hot, I will spue thee out of my mouth.* I was, it seemed, just going to church for show. From **Revelation 3:20** *Behold, I stand at the door, and knock: if any man hear my voice, and open the door, I will come in to him, and will sup with him, and he with me.* Jesus was knocking at the door of my heart, just waiting for me to realize that I needed him. He had been the *man* that I needed all the time! I opened the door to my heart and it seemed that right then and there I could hear the hammer hitting the chisel, and feel the chipping away at the excess baggage full of flaws, sin, and evil "stuff."

Cursing was the biggest piece of luggage I found. I was better than the best at it because I wanted to fit in. I had what one of my brothers would call a "potty mouth," although I never cursed around any of them. One day I was walking (I don't know why because I had a car) and this woman just seemed to appear. I didn't know her, had never seen her before, and never saw her again. To this day, I don't know where this woman came from. It all seemed like it could have been a dream, but indeed it was a wake-up call! She approached me, first complimenting me, saying I was such a pretty girl and how nice I looked, but she couldn't see how I ate with "that mouth." I was smiling and giddy from the compliments until I realized I wasn't understanding what she was saying. I was still stuck on the "such a pretty girl" part. I demonstrated how I ate, gesturing. She said, "No, baby, I mean how can you eat with all that filth coming out of your mouth? I can look at you and tell your mother didn't raise you like that!" Oh, how right she was! My mother certainly did not raise me like that. I was so embarrassed, those curse words ceased to exist in my vocabulary almost immediately. She had to have been one of those angels watching over me, because I never saw her before or since that day in 1974. God has His way of putting us where we need to be for our highest good. Even then I never walked alone because God was there all the time, working on me and waiting.

The chisels were still chipping at my lying, adultery against God, the search for love, and making others and things my gods; all these things were weighing me down. The chiseling was working on the shell I had covered my heart with, so as not to be hurt, but I still hurt so inside.

The desires of my heart that did not include God began to fall to the ground and I mean in huge pieces. There were nails, nailing my faults to the cross (see the prints in His hands and feet?), and the paint (his blood streaming down all over me), that covered the "old me." **Romans 12:1-2** *I beseech you therefore, brethren, by the mercies of God, that ye present your bodies a living sacrifice, holy, acceptable unto God, which is your reasonable service. And be not conformed to this world: but be ye transformed by the renewing of your mind, that ye may prove what is that good, and acceptable, and perfect, will of God.* Also, here again, **II Corinthians 5:17** *Therefore if any man be in Christ, he is a new creature: old things are passed away; behold, all things are become new.* God, made me over in giving me the mind to present my body to Him, a living sacrifice, instead of to man, and to refresh my thoughts He showed me **Philippians 2:5** *Let this mind be in you, which was also in Christ Jesus*: and **Philippians 4:8** *Finally, brethren, whatsoever things are true, whatsoever things are honest, whatsoever things are just, whatsoever things are pure, whatsoever things are lovely, whatsoever things are of good report; if there be any virtue, and if there be any praise,* ***think on these things****.*

God chose me to choose Him (**John 15:16a** *Ye have not chosen me, but I have chosen you*), and I decided to follow Jesus. I made a change from bar hopping to church hopping, attending women's conferences as often as they became available. I gained a thirst for God's Word until it became (and still is) a part of my daily living (**Matthew 5:6** *Blessed are they which do hunger and thirst after righteousness: for they shall be filled*). I attended Bible classes at the churches that my church fellowshipped with so that I was in Bible classes Monday through Wednesday, feasting on the Word. I learned to pray and spend time in His Word before going to work. I would get up extra early just for my "God time." I could feel a change in me, no longer searching for what I could not find without Him.

At forty-two, on Palm Sunday, April 8, 1990, I was singing the song "Lead Me to Calvary":

"*Lest I forget Gethsemane, lest I forget thine agony; lest I forget thy love for me, lead me to Calvary.*"

The Lord did just that! He led me to view the cross where He died for me and for all mankind. A change, a change had come over me; He changed my life and made me free. What a glorious day that was! Salvation had come to my house!!!

I challenge you: What is the weight that so easily besets you and is weighing you down and preventing you from having joy? What are you in search of that leads you to heaviness of heart and no peace within? What is the weight that you carry so deeply that you cannot run to Christ crying, "What must I do to be saved?" Have you thought about laying in "wait" on the Lord? God allowed me to change from carrying the weight of excess baggage to waiting in Him and on Him. He can do the same for you, too!

In all that Job went through, what God allowed Him to go through, his response was **Job 14:14** *If a man die, shall he live again? All the days of my appointed time will I* ***wait****, till my change come.* **Isaiah 40:31** *But they that* ***wait*** *upon the Lord shall renew their strength; they shall mount up with wings as eagles; they shall run, and not be weary; and they shall walk, and not faint.* **Psalm 27:14**

Wait *on the Lord: be of good courage, and he shall strengthen thine heart:* **wait***, I say, on the Lord.*

In **II Timothy 3:16** these words can be found and oh how true they are: *All scripture is given by inspiration of God, and is profitable for doctrine, for reproof, for correction, for instruction in righteousness.* Through reading and studying the Word of God, He gave me an extreme makeover by the blood of His Son, Jesus Christ. And now I'm not the same, because everything has changed, all because of Christ.

Just as I am, and waiting not; To rid my soul of one dark blot,
To Thee whose blood can cleanse each spot, O Lamb of God, I come! I come!

CHAPTER 5

THIS IS MY STORY, THIS IS MY SONG, PART I

"I" NEVER WALKED ALONE

> When you walk through a storm, hold your head up high
> And don't be afraid of the dark; At the end of the storm,
> there's a golden sky, And the sweet, silver song of a lark
> Walk on through the wind, Walk on through the rain
> Though your dreams be tossed and blown
> Walk on, walk on, with hope in your heart
> and you'll never walk alone. You'll never walk alone.
>
> *Lyrics by Richard Rodgers and Oscar Hammerstein,*
> *music by Richard Rodgers (1945)*

I chose these lyrics because even when I didn't know the Lord, He was there all of the time. I never walked alone, **never**!

Through the years, I kept on toiling, toiling through storms and rain, but I never lost my faith. I married my first husband on September 14, 1999, and oh, the joy that floods my soul. (I had been through the ceremony before, but my husband now is my first husband.) It is so great to be "equally yoked with a believer." We met through the John Eberhart Community Chorus, of which we are now both members, singing praises to God together.

Some twenty years have passed and I have developed a relationship with the Lord. Oh, hallelujah! I get frightened when I think of my past and how I was living my life. I think of those many years from childhood to adulthood. I think of the choices I made and it seems that too many of them were bad choices, but scripture reminds me in **Proverbs 21:2** *Every way of a man is right in his own eyes: but the Lord pondereth the hearts* (God knows our hearts and our hearts' intentions). You see, I thought I had it going on, as the old saying goes. It seemed that I was doing things right. I was going "to" church every Sunday (as so many of us do), yet the church was not in me. That is the case with many of us in our daily lives; in our careers, if our hearts aren't in what we do, our production is down. We are dissatisfied, we want change, but **we don't want to change**. I was making the same mistakes over and over. I often think, *How could I have ever thought of being without God in my life?* To God Be The Glory (TGBTG) for the things He has done, for the things He is doing in my life now and for the things that are to come.

As I tell my story, I praise God for my relationship with Him. I mean, I am a real church girl now, and a helpmeet to my husband. We are in church, Sunday school, mission, Bible class every week and here comes Satan in for the . . . . Hey! If God is for me, who or what can be against me?

I mean, that *is* what is written in **Romans 8:31** *What shall we then say to these things? If God be for us, who can be against us?*

When I think back to when my mother was going through her battle with cancer, I thought, *There is no way in the world I would go through chemotherapy and radiation treatments and be this sick.* But she did it for her family. As women, we are the nurturers of the family. We fight for our families at all costs. We strive for strength to endure whatever comes our way in order to be there for them, and as children of the King, we are trusting in Him to the end. I said earlier that Mom always told me, "Take care of your dad and your brother." Perhaps she saw that death was inevitable and wanted to be reassured that they would be okay after she was gone. I told her that I would take care of them and, along with my brothers, I took care of Dad until he passed some twenty-seven years later, and my brothers and I are all still looking after each other.

As my mother struggled to live for us, she still trusted in God; her courage showed in her smiles through her pain, and her faith was evident in her testimony of "no fear, because God knows what He is doing." I was encouraged through a cousin of mine who called and read me **Psalm 23:4** *Yea, though I walk through the valley of the shadow of death, I will fear no evil: for thou art with me; thy rod and thy staff they comfort me.* That scripture would come back to my remembrance as I went through my battles. Even with that it was difficult to watch her slipping away. In fact, I asked God to take her and He didn't. Now I had an attitude when He did and had the nerve to think in my heart, *I told you to take her before, when I felt I was ready for her to leave me and you didn't! Why did you take her now?* God is so good because He could have taken me and left her here, but His grace and mercy allowed me to live on, for He had plans for my life, as in **Jeremiah 29:11** *For I know the thoughts that I think toward you, saith the Lord, thoughts of peace, and not of evil, to give you an expected end.*

Fast-forward to March 2010, as I prepared for retirement. I could start drawing Social Security three months before my sixty-second birthday, which would be on June 24, 2010. My plans were to keep working part-time as a nurse escort on the school bus for medically fragile and special needs children, something I truly loved doing. Special needs—wow! We all have special needs; after all, we are special to God, we are His children. With the extra income, I had plans to do some things around the house. My husband and I would be able to take some nice trips and attend all of the Christian education functions. You name it, it was in the plans, *my* plans!

Another "Job moment" was on its way. We know the history of Job's challenges. Now I can go along with all of the "that there is none like him (her) on the earth, but a perfect and upright "wo-man." I was and still am striving to be perfect and upright. (**Job 1:8**). I can agree that, yes, I feared God and I try to avoid evil, and there isn't another being like me; I believe that God created us in the same way, but with our own uniqueness, personality, and heart.

When I went for a physical, I was asked when I had my last colonoscopy. I said, "A long time ago and it wasn't even done the way they are today." You were wide awake and knew exactly what was going on and it was not a comfortable position to be in. So I had a colonoscopy and received a call, telling me that my results were suspicious, there was a small ulcer. A biopsy showed cancer cells. In my prayer journal from April 15, 2010, I wrote, "I don't quite remember what the doctor said, but I remember that the word 'cancer' didn't seem to phase me. Perhaps subconsciously I suspected that, but all the while was hoping it wasn't. I thank you, Lord, for the peace that passes all understanding." I thought, *Now Jesus, this is not what I had in "my" plans, but, okay, what's next?* In May 2010, I had surgery to remove the cancer. According to the medical board requirements, twelve lymph nodes were removed and biopsied for any further cancer. One lymph node came back positive, which meant that I would have to undergo chemotherapy treatments. I thought in my mind, *That must have been the one closest to the ulcer/cancer, so I am good.* As a nurse, we have a tendency to diagnose and make our own prognoses. I again thought back to my mom and her treatments; on June 5, 2010, I wrote in my prayer journal at 7:29 a.m., saying (literally) "Dear Lord, I am like Jesus now, when He was in the Garden praying." **Matthew 26:39** *And he went a little further, and fell on His face, and prayed, saying, O my Father, if it be possible, let this cup pass from me: nevertheless not as I will, but as thou wilt.* I meant that prayer with the utmost sincerity.

I was not liking what was happening to me and I wanted "that cup" to pass; however, I thought, *If this is your plan, God, then not my will, but Thine be done. And O God, I ask that you prepare me for your Will.* My prayer was literally, "Jesus, Jesus, Jesus"—sometimes when you don't know what to pray for, you can just call on the name of Jesus, and I did. I think now, as I write, about **Romans 8:26-27** *Likewise the Spirit also helpeth our infirmities: for we know not what we should pray for as we ought: but the Spirit itself maketh intercession for us with groanings which cannot be uttered. And he that searcheth the hearts knoweth what is the mind of the Spirit, because he maketh intercession for the saints according to the will of God.* I praise God for His Holy Spirit.

I went into prayer mode—which I try to be in most of the time for anything and everything—and I sent out a call for prayers from the north, south, east, and west, especially to my family and friends, my pastor and his wife, the Reverend Robert B. Jones Sr. and Sister Bernice, and without a doubt, Sweet Kingdom Missionary Baptist Church, my church family. I thank God for all of you! I truly believe the scripture **James 5:16b** *The effectual fervent prayer of a righteous man availeth much.* I remembered that I had prayed and asked God that if I ever had to go through anything, I wanted to be in the same spiritual frame of mind as my mother had been. I wanted strength, I wanted courage, I had faith and it didn't take a whole lot. **Matthew 17:20** *And Jesus said unto them, Because of your unbelief: for verily I say unto you, If ye have faith as a grain of mustard seed, ye shall say unto this mountain, Remove hence to yonder place; and it shall remove; and nothing shall be impossible unto you.*

That colon cancer was a mountain, but somehow—and I don't know how—God assured me that it was not a death sentence, as we often think when we hear the word cancer. That mountain was removed by "faith as a grain of mustard seed." I was good at accepting the treatment recommendations; however, I was so outdone! That is to say, cancer was not in my plans! Let me just say here: we have to remember who God is and "whose" we are. We have to remember that He is in charge! God has His way of doing what He does. Remember my plans to keep working after retirement, draw social security, and make extra income? I had to have chemotherapy every two weeks for six months, and I had to quit working because my immune system would be compromised. I would not be able to work with the sick or with children. What? *Hmmmm*, I thought, **my** *plans*. **Jeremiah 29:11** came to mind again, from the **New Living Translation**: *"For I know the plans I have for you," says the Lord. "They are plans for good and not for disaster, to give you a future and a hope."*

All the while I faced these challenges that were never in my plans, I never walked alone. While still in the hospital, during the daytime I was preoccupied with the TV, visitors, doctors making rounds, and nurses. At midnight, you might call for help and no one heard you . . . but God . . . but God . . . but God! Remember Paul and Silas? **Acts 16:25 *And at midnight*** *Paul and Silas prayed, and sang praises unto God: and the prisoners heard them.* I would hum, "Jesus, Jesus, Jesus; Jesus, Jesus, Jesus; Jesus, Jesus, Jesus; Jesus, Jesus, Jesus." Jesus was the whole song. Tears began to come, but as I hummed the tune, they stopped. As I continued to hum, God made His presence known as only He can. I felt, it seemed, my bed beginning to move from side to side, as if He were rocking me to sleep. I remember comfort coming and thinking, *Yes, Jesus loves me, for the Bible tells me so*. It was as if I had crawled up in His lap and He comforted me. **Psalm 23:4** *Yea, though I walk through the valley of the shadow of death, I will fear no evil: for thou art with me; thy rod and thy staff they comfort me.* When I think of this scripture, I think of the word "through." *Yea though I walk through* . . . this ministered to me greatly because "through" seemed to indicate movement, meaning I wasn't staying at that point. I was "moving through a valley of displeasure." How pleasant is the Word of God in times like these. "Be very sure your anchor holds and grips The Solid Rock." Even then, God brought His Word to my remembrance. Thank you, Jesus!

I thought, *What am I going to do now? I can't work and I can't work my plans.* I received comfort through His Word, as in **Isaiah 55:8** *For my thoughts are not your thoughts, neither are your ways my ways, saith the Lord.* Oh, how quickly I learned "life application" of his Word. **Isaiah 26:3** *Thou wilt keep him in perfect peace, whose mind is stayed on thee: because he trusteth in thee.* **Philippians 4:7** *And the peace of God, which passeth all understanding, shall keep your hearts and minds through Christ Jesus.* He ministered to me in scripture, one after another: **II Chronicles 20:15 (in part)** *Thus saith the Lord unto you, be not afraid nor dismayed by reason of this great multitude; for the battle is not yours, but God's.*

Satan thought he had a battle going on with me, but it was with God, and God won. On 11/11/11 (November 11, 2011), I was given a clean bill of health. As Satan was with Jesus, tempting him, **Luke 4:13** *And when the devil had ended all the temptation, he departed from him for a season,* he too left me for a season.

During that time, like Job, in my spirit I could sense others wondering why I was going through these health challenges. Suggestions were being offered about what I should do: eat this or drink that. "Take this vitamin" or "Have you tried herbs?" and "What did you do for this to come on you?" I appreciated all the concern, but not once did I ever have a command from the Holy Spirit to do anything other than what I was doing or what I was being told to do by my medical team. I truly believe that I was just a chosen vessel of God for His glory as in **John 9:3** *Jesus answered, Neither hath this man sinned, nor his parents: but that the works of God should be made manifest in him.* Through it all, prayer was all around me. My cousin Deac would call me regularly and pray with me. My aunt in Georgia would call before each treatment and pray with me. I have a praying family and church family, true men and women of God.

My medical team was hand-picked by the Master Himself! Every one of my doctors were Christians and did not hesitate to agree with me when I let them know Who was in charge and that I was a praying "sista." God gave me that blessed assurance that I have never walked alone, as in **Hebrews 13:5b** . . . *for he hath said, I will never leave thee, nor forsake thee.*

Never Alone

When in affliction's valley; I'm treading the road of care,
My Savior helps me to carry; My cross when heavy to bear,
Though all around me is darkness, Earthly joys all flown;
My Savior whispers His promise, "I never will leave thee alone."
No, never alone, No, never alone, He promised never to leave me,
never to leave me alone.

(Public domain)

CHAPTER 6

THIS IS MY STORY, THIS IS MY SONG, PART II

I'VE BEEN THROUGH THE STORM AND THE RAIN, BUT I MADE IT

After receiving the clean bill of health in November 2011, I thought, *All is well and it is smooth sailing.*

Going into the new year, 2012, many times during night-watch services, I would listen to the testimonies of many who would talk about the trials and tribulations that God had brought them through and I would think, *I'm not going to say anything because mine ain't as good as theirs.* I thought this way because I often heard it asked, "Does anybody have a testimony? And I am not talking about losing your car keys!" I thought that meant you needed an exciting testimony, so I kept my car key stories to myself, even though I knew that it could have meant losing my job if I didn't find them to get to work on time. Every day that I woke up was a testimony, but I didn't realize that until years later.

Many years ago, as I entered the parking structure on my way to work, my car caught on fire and I didn't know it until a woman banged on my window, yelling, "Get out, your car is on fire!" The flames were coming from under the car. I stepped out of the car into the flames, but I didn't get burned or even singed.

How amazing! I remember driving home to Port Huron one winter night in heavy snow. I thought, *I'm good*, because I was listening to my cassette player and singing along to church songs. A truck in front of me appeared to be stopping so I slowed down; but as I watched, it didn't even seem to be moving anymore, so I started tapping my brakes. Because of the slippery road, I went into a spin and saw myself headed toward a ditch and a telephone pole, thinking I was going to wrap around that pole. I remember saying, "JE . . . SUS!" There is something about that name! I ended up in the ditch, stopped beside that pole, headed in the opposite direction, only able to see the tires of cars as they passed by. Thank you, Jesus! I thought, *Doesn't anyone see me in this ditch?* No one was stopping. It was dark and my lights were on. *Don't they see me? Isn't anyone going to help me?* I said, "Okay, Lord, I need you to get me out of here." He did! I moved the car back and forward twice and on the third time (in the name of the Father, Son, and Holy Ghost), I spun out of the ditch, heading back in the direction I was going and I started singing, "No, Never Alone." As I was singing I saw what looked like a person in a white hooded robe going into a building (could that have been? Naa! But God!), and thought, *And he didn't even come to help me?* These testimonies never reached the church for a couple reasons. First, I was so blown away by them myself that I figured no one would ever believe me; and second, I went to find the ditch the next day and I couldn't. The building wasn't there, either. Was it a dream or vision? Or was it just my imagination, running away with me?

As I look back over my life and I think things over, I have a testimony. In hindsight, both incidents were God getting my attention, letting me know that I had to tell someone about Him. Every day that He allows me to breathe His air is a testimony of His goodness, grace, and mercy.

Lamentations 3:21-23 *This I recall to my mind, therefore have I hope. It is of the Lord's mercies that we are not consumed, because His compassions fail not. They* ***are new every morning****: great is thy faithfulness.*

Every day that God allows you to breathe His air you ought to tell somebody, for it is a testimony! Every day He allows you to awaken in your right mind is a testimony and you ought to tell somebody! What may seem trivial to you or to some may be just the encouragement needed for another to come to Christ.

When God allowed me to come through the challenges of lichen planus, the skin disorder I had (and it still comes out on occasion, I guess as a reminder of where I have been), and through the ordeal of colon cancer, I gave Him praise. He has been with me through it all and I have learned to depend upon His Word. When we give our testimonies, we have His Word that encourages us. It can be sickness, it can be the death of loved ones, anything that changes "our planning"—and rather than lose hope we can hear our Heavenly Father ministering to us through His Word.

It is often said that God does not talk to us, or so we think; but when you become a lover of His Word, He brings it back to your remembrance at the right time and in time. You may even hear Him in another's voice giving you encouragement by His Word. Listen. Listen. Listen! You will find yourself in a conversation with Him when you least expect it. He does hear and answer prayers. **Psalm 91:15** *He shall call upon me, and I will answer him: I will be with him in trouble; I will deliver him, and honour him.* **Isaiah 65:24** *And it shall come to pass, that before they call, I will answer; and while they are yet speaking, I will hear.* **Jeremiah 33:3** *Call unto me, and I will answer thee, and shew thee great and mighty things, which thou knowest not.* Get into God's Word and let His Word get into you for life application. You're talking about a relationship beyond what we can ever think or ask. **Ephesians 3:20** *Now unto him that is able to do exceeding abundantly above all that we ask or think, according to the power that worketh in us.* I tell you it is in His Word!

As I said at the beginning of this chapter, I thought at the time, *All is well and there's nothing but smooth sailing ahead. I have a testimony and I am moving right along.* Fast forward to January 2013.

Ladies, ladies, ladies: This is not only my testimony, but health advice as well. Being a nurse for over forty years, I learned some things, I guess you could say, and as a cancer survivor, I tune in more to things that happen. We are all getting older and some say wiser, which is my hope, particularly about getting wiser. Don't let your busy-ness hinder your business. Look after yourselves. Annual exams are important—mammograms and Pap smears. If you don't have insurance, many agencies offer free screenings, so there is no excuse and fear is not an option. I was told by an evangelist years ago that fear is an acronym for **F**alse **E**vidence **A**ppearing **R**eal. That is how Satan works. He tries to steal your joy by telling you things that are not real, and we have a tendency to believe him as though they were.

Every sickness and health challenge is not unto death. If you see something out of the norm for you, handle your business! Early detection is vital to health issues and challenges. Seek out health care providers that have a love for life and those that will work diligently toward your health.

Here I was, planning again, and I know that I consulted God beforehand. He reminded me of **Jeremiah 29:11** *For I know the thoughts that I think toward you, saith the Lord, thoughts of peace, and not of evil, to give you an expected end,* (again in the **NIV Translation**) *For I know the plans I have for you," declares the Lord, "plans to prosper you and not to harm you, plans to give you hope and a future*).

In January 2013, I decided I was tired of hair relaxers and applying chemicals to my hair, so I went back to wearing a short natural. Is anyone hearing me in this? Was God preparing me with my hair for what was to come?

In January, I also went for my annual Pap smear. Menopause had kicked in in November 1999 and all of a sudden Mother Nature was starting to show her face again. What? I mean, what is this? The Pap smear came back "not positive but not negative" either. I had to have a more extensive exam under anesthesia.

For whatever reason, I was not given that exam until June; however in March 2013, I received notice that I would qualify for Medicare effective the first of the month that I would be turning sixty-five! Hallelujah! To God be the glory! *What a blessing*, I thought, not knowing it would be coming in right on time! Look at God! Medicare kicked in on June 1, 2013 and I was scheduled to have a D & C (dilatation and curettage) on Saturday, June 15, 2013. I received a call on June 18, 2013, stating that the exam showed uterine cancer. I thought, *Aw man! Here we go again. God saying to Satan, 'Have you considered my servant, Wilma?' Hadn't I been considered enough yet? How was I going to tell my BabyDoll and the rest of my family, my brothers, my children, all who had been through the colon cancer journey with me?* "Help me, Holy Ghost, in the name of Jesus," was my immediate prayer.

Let's back up a bit. I had had a fibroid uterus from the age of thirty-five and was told that if it didn't bother me, the doctors wouldn't bother it. I was fine with that. I wanted to leave here with everything I came with. That is not always a good reason. The cancer had settled in those fibroids. Ladies, ladies, ladies: check yourselves! Fibroids can be removed if caught early enough. For those who want children, it's not always necessary to have a hysterectomy. (If you want more information, please call or e-mail me.)

On June 19, 2013, another physician called me to come into his office right away. I thought, *Dear God, what is going on here? This must really be serious this time.* I thought I would take my BabyDoll with me and the doctor could tell him and answer his questions; my husband has a gift of asking the right questions and I thought, *Who better to explain?* We went to see the doctor the same evening he called. He explained how the cancer was not detected in the Pap smear. He scheduled a CT scan for me for June 21. Wow! The doctor actually called to schedule the test. *This has really got to be serious,* I thought, *because usually the receptionist or nurse scheduled these tests.* I had the test done and the doctor called me with the good news that it had not spread anywhere else, **but** "we need to do surgery immediately." It was Friday; the doctor wanted to schedule my surgery for the next Monday, which was June 24, at 7:00 a.m. Okay now—here "I" go! "I don't think so, because that is my birthday and I am going to be celebrating sixty-five and Medicare!" There was a pause over the phone. The doctor repeated himself and I repeated myself, saying, "Monday is my birthday and having surgery that day is not going to make for a good birthday gift!" He agreed and scheduled it for the following Monday.

I ask this question again of you, "Is anybody hearing me in this?" My health insurance had ended in March, and Medicare started June 1, 2013. Look at God! Look at God! Look at God! Remember the old saying, "There's some good in everything that is bad and there's some bad in everything that is good?" The bad news was needed to have the surgery for cancer; the good news was having the insurance to cover it! Look at God! Look at God! Look at God! **Philippians 4:19** *But my God shall supply all your need according to His riches in glory by Christ Jesus.*

I didn't know about the future, but I knew who held my hand, for you see, I never walked alone. God was and is with me all the time. I never felt like He wasn't with me; even when I didn't know Him, and probably didn't want to know Him—he was there even then.

I was hospitalized for a week. I received excellent care and again it seemed at "midnight" that I would awaken to discomfort, but I was able to climb up in the lap of Jesus, my Lord and Savior, and lay my head upon His breast. I could hear Him in His Word, **Matthew 11:28** *Come unto me, all ye that labour and are heavy laden, and I will give you rest.* In His presence, I remembered **Isaiah 26:3** *Thou wilt keep him in perfect peace, whose mind is stayed on thee: because he trusteth in thee.*

Are you trusting in God, in His Son Jesus Christ, and the Holy Spirit? **Philippians 4:7** *And the peace of God, which passeth all understanding, shall keep your hearts and minds through Christ Jesus.* When it seems that all is tumbling down around you, don't give in; give yourself up to God (**Hebrews 12:2a** *Looking unto Jesus the author and finisher of our faith*).

I don't know about tomorrow; but I know who holds my hand . . .

On July 8, I was discharged from the hospital.

CHAPTER 7

THIS IS MY STORY, THIS IS MY SONG, PART III

OH, TO BE KEPT BY JESUS, KEPT BY HIS POWER DIVINE

It is so wonderful to be in the care of a loving Father, a loving God. In the previous chapter, I closed with this statement: On **July 8**, I came home from the hospital. On **July 9**, 2013, my husband was admitted to the hospital for knee-replacement surgery. I tell his story because of what God did for me while I watched my husband go through a valley leading to unfamiliar territory, seeming to see me as a stranger. I was in a "strange land" watching my husband, my BabyDoll, but God gave me a song to sing. Through it all, I learned to depend upon His Word.

You see, I couldn't go with my husband for the surgery because I had just been discharged myself. I went to see him the day after his surgery, July 10, 2013. Our sisters were there with him, but I needed to see him for myself. My brother took me and picked me up. That was and still is my husband, my BabyDoll, and I felt a strong need to be his helpmeet when he couldn't help himself. I couldn't do much, but I could get on the nerves of the people who could do something when things weren't looking the way "I, the nurse" thought they should.

During his recovery, unfortunately, he had a negative reaction to medication. I noticed him looking at me strangely, kind of like "a foolish woman" (like Job's wife). He started telling me various things that were not accurate, and he looked at me, not really knowing who I was—and I had a major problem with that! He wasn't calling me by my name and when I kissed him on the cheeks he looked at me like "who are you?" I went home for the day in major prayer mode.

One night while he was still an inpatient, I received a call from the hospital (as it was coming up on midnight, another Paul and Silas moment), telling me my husband was in intensive care. He was in critical condition, with a fever high enough that he needed a cooling blanket. Praise God it was not His "cooling board!" There is something about midnight. I immediately went into prayer while talking to the Master Physician. I said, "Lord, I am not ready for you to take my BabyDoll, and I need for you to step in as only you can and bring my husband back to me and back to his right mind. He doesn't know me and that is a problem!

"I need you, Lord Jesus, I need you right now."

I waited until the "sixth hour" and began making phone calls, apologizing as I talked to my cousin, Pastor Carl, for calling so early. I said, "I don't need you to come down from Port Huron, but I need you to pray. I told him what was going on and prayer was on! I e-mailed the Council of Baptist Pastors, of which my husband was a member, and told them we needed their prayers. I e-mailed Pastor Lindsey, the pastor who married us.

Now this was truly God working on my behalf! In the e-mail I had asked Pastor Lindsey to call me because my "BabyDoll" was in intensive care at Receiving Hospital. That e-mail went out at 7:02 a.m.; visiting hours didn't start until 8:00 a.m. and I was there, waiting. To my surprise, one of the pastors from the council was coming into the room and Pastor Lindsey was coming up the hall. He told me I'd forgotten to leave the phone number, so he just came over. Look at God! I am again reminded of **Isaiah 65:24** *And it shall come to pass, that before they call, I will answer; and while they are yet speaking, I* *will hear.* In my weakness, God was working and sent the men of God to the hospital. When I walked into his room after receiving that midnight call, my husband was alert! Hallelujah! I asked if he knew who I was and he said, "Yes, my BabyDoll, and where have you been?" I was so thrilled to hear that, because he hadn't known me for four days. Prayer does change things and, many times, right before our eyes.

Satan has his way of coming at us from any angle he can and with whatever he thinks can bring the "children of God" down. You see, he is still angry at God for kicking him out of heaven and is trying hard to get back at him through us, God's children. By whatever means he can, he will try it all.

I couldn't imagine both of us being down at the same time; I mean, who was going to take care of whom? God saw us through with the help of many family members and friends. What a mighty God we serve!

Satan got busy again, this time working on us through our children. When my husband and I married, we brought together my son, his two sons and two daughters, along with my "plus" children, another two daughters and a son. Together we were the proud parents of eight children, grandparents of thirteen, and great-grandparents of three. When we would all come together, it was always great family fun.

I was going through another chemotherapy session for the uterine cancer. Our oldest son lived in Chicago, but would call regularly to check on us. He always wanted to know, "Ma are you doing okay? I just wanted to hear your voice and check on you and Daddy." I would ask how he was because he always sounded so short of breath. He always told me, "I'm good." Little did we know the condition of his health, and the condition of his heart. God called his name and he answered on September 11, 2013. I did not give birth to Darryl, but he was **our** oldest son. It was such devastating news to receive, so hard to handle, so hard to believe! What do you do? You definitely don't expect to outlive your children! A link in the family chain had been broken.

We wonder at times, "Why, God? Why our son?" and the thought always comes to mind, "You gave your only Son for us, for the world, for our sin." I heard a statement made recently, "Even our children are not ours, but yours, Lord"—so very true. **Psalm 24:1** (A Psalm of David) *The earth is the Lord's, and the fullness thereof; the world, and **they** that dwell therein.* From **Ezekiel 18:4** in part . . . *Behold, **all souls** are mine; as the soul of the Father, so also the soul of the son is mine...* Our comfort was in knowing that he had a relationship with God and according to **I Thessalonians 4:16-17** *For the Lord Himself shall descend from heaven with a shout, with the voice of the archangel, and with the trump of God: and the dead in Christ shall rise first: Then we which are alive and remain shall be caught up together with them in the clouds, to meet the Lord in the air: and so shall we ever be with the Lord.*

Romans 8:28 *And we know that all things work together for good to them that love God, to them who are the called according to His purpose* (our "expected end").

CHAPTER 8

MANY THINGS ABOUT TOMORROW WE DON'T SEEM TO UNDERSTAND

So—we made some lemonade with the lemons that were tossed our way. We added the sweetness of Jesus and we have tasted and seen that the Lord, He is good. **Psalm 34:8** *O taste and see that the Lord is good:* **blessed is the man that trusteth in Him.**

Now we were headed in for the last stretch of the year. Chemotherapy seemed to be going well. I'd lost all of my hair, but, "Honey, just call me Sister Ko-jacky, I'm still cute!" "Yes you are," some would agree. That was the way I prepared my church family and friends. I did not have a problem with losing my hair at all. *I* was still here! When I went to church for the first time and had to take off my hat to sing in the choir, my very dear friend (trying to cover her feelings) said, "Here comes "baldy-locks." We laughed together for real. Some may think that was pretty cold, but you had to know us and our relationship to appreciate it. I was glad to hear her joke rather than see her tears and pity.

I had warned my family that this time around I would lose my hair, and I did. I remember going to sing with the community choir one Saturday late in the fall and I took off my hat. I could see their concern for me, so I asked the choir members, "Does anyone have a comb? This one strand of hair will not lay right and I need to comb it down." They were cracking up and it broke the ice of their discomfort for me. It did not keep me from singing, "Order My Steps" or "All Night, All Day, Angels Watching Over Me". I took photos of my progressive hair growth and labeled the pictures "Hair by Christ" and He did my eyebrows, too! I had never worn a wig before in my life. In fact, as a child they seemed rather scary to me and I wanted no part of them, not even for Halloween. Losing my hair was not an embarrassment to me; it meant that I still had life. It meant that I was receiving another opportunity to tell someone about Jesus, He who was keeping me through it all. It meant that I was still His and He was still in charge of me.

I bowled in a Christian league and was captain of my team at that time. One evening, it was my turn to bowl and I was going to roll a strike! Not! The ball literally dropped from my hand and I couldn't move; my brother practically carried me to my seat. What happened? An indescribable pain on the left side of my back would not let me move. How could a pain on the left side affect the use of my right hand and arm? Of course I called on Jesus, the designer in charge.

Wow! Do we really realize the beauty of our being? **Psalm 139:14** *I will praise thee; for I am fearfully and wonderfully made: marvelous are thy works; and that my soul knoweth right well.*

God's design of man is so intricately that man cannot duplicate man, no matter how learned he may be, and yet it amazes me that the same man wants to plant the seed that "things just happen." That God had nothing to do with our creation and our likeness to Him. How is that? Every detail of our being in the beginning was pre-ordained. **Romans 8:29-30** *For whom he did foreknow, he also did predestinate to be conformed to the image of His Son, that he might be the firstborn among many brethren. Moreover whom he did predestinate, them he also called: and whom he called, them he also justified: and whom he justified, them he also glorified.*

Here comes Satan again and God is saying, "Have you considered my servant Wilma again?" God, haven't I been considered enough? Nevertheless, not my will but Thine be done . . .

On December 30, 2013, I went to the emergency room for severe back pain. I was released, but I had to go back in for emergency surgery on New Year's Day. The problem had progressed so that I was unable to walk without assistance. What a way to ring in the New Year! Some say that the way you bring in the New Year is how you will spend the remainder of the year. Given my history with cancer, something was discovered growing on my spine and the doctors treated it as if it were a tumor and did a biopsy. Praise God, an MRI showed that it was just a herniated disc, and the biopsy proved to be noncancerous. I was there for a few days, again asking God to help me through it all. As I went through physical therapy to get back in shape, I began to think, *This is not supposed to be happening to me. I am supposed to be the helper, not the one being helped.*

No matter what we go through, there is a reason for it. It is a test of our faith, an opportunity to witness about Jesus, and we learn that God is taking us through and we are not alone. This kept my mind off my discomfort and it confirmed **Isaiah 26:3** *Thou wilt keep him in perfect peace, whose mind is stayed on thee: because he trusteth in thee.* There is none like our Heavenly Father. TGBTG: To God Be The Glory! He healed my body again and I was out and about once more, ready to begin February with a bang!

God, you have got to be kidding! I went back to the emergency room with a threatening bowel obstruction. It was a bit unsettling that the people at the hospital were getting to know me. The staff was asking, "Weren't you just here?" I had only one more chemotherapy treatment, but it kept being postponed by other health issues. Here came Satan, but God won again. I gave out a call to the prayer warriors, this time nearly in tears because, "God, I don't want to be cut again. Help me, Holy Ghost!" God heard my cry and dried my tears. I wasn't afraid; I just didn't want to be hurting anymore.

The doctors said the bowel obstruction was probably due to scar tissue from previous surgeries and the chemotherapy treatments; if it didn't move on its own they would have to do surgery because of its size. I thank God and His angels for keeping watch over me. I was in the hospital for four days before the obstruction moved at God's command. It was a great day for praising the Lord. Though the obstruction moved, it **was** an ordeal because again, I was thinking about my plans. Had I not learned yet that God was in control and that everything that was and is happens for a reason? At the time I was working on getting "our" first book published. My goal was to have it completed by my birthday. Needless to say, it came out in God's time and I was happy and healthy to receive it.

We don't always have to know the reasons why, but be willing to go through the valleys that God is allowing us to go through, knowing that He is not surprised and He is going through them with us.

I don't know about tomorrow, I just live from day to day. I don't borrow from its sunshine, for its skies may turn to gray. I don't worry o'er the future for I know what Jesus said, and today I'll walk beside Him for he knows what is ahead.
Ira F. Stanphill 1950

'Tis so sweet to trust in Jesus, just to take Him at His Word, just to rest upon His promise, just to know, "Thus saith the Lord." Jesus, Jesus, how I trust Him! How I've proved Him o'er and o'er! Jesus, Jesus, precious Jesus! O for grace to trust Him more.
(Louisa M. R. Stead, c1850-1917, William James Kirkpatrick, 1838-1921)

As I remembered my plans for me, this scripture comes to mind: **James 4:13-15** *Go to now, ye that say, To day or to morrow we will go into such a city, and continue there a year, and buy and sell, and get gain: Whereas ye know not what shall be on the morrow. For what is your life? It is even a vapour, that appeareth for* *a little time, and then vanisheth away. For that ye ought to say,* **If the Lord will***, we shall live, and do this, or that.*

This is not to say that we shouldn't plan, but our planning should include "if the Lord will" in it. His will shall be done, whether we are in agreement or not. His will shall be done, whether we like it or not; it is not our call. He knows what is best for us and He is liberal in His giving to the extent that we are to give Him the glory that is due Him and not man. I guess it is kind of like, "Don't forget to remember where all of our blessings come from."

CHAPTER 9

WHETHER I LIVE OR DIE, I WIN!

II Corinthians 5:8 *We are confident, I say, and willing rather to be absent from the body, and to be present with the Lord.*

As I look back over my life and just the past four years, I truly have had many testimonies and I can only say, "TGBTG: To God Be The Glory." Some have said, "I had no idea you went through all of that." The key words are "went through." And it really was but a light thing in comparison to those I met along the way in my journey. **II Corinthians 4:15-18** *For all things are for your sakes, that the abundant grace might through the thanksgiving of many redound to the glory of God. For which cause we faint not; but though our outward man perish, yet the inward man is renewed day by day. For* **our light affliction**, *which is but for a moment, worketh for us a far more exceeding and eternal weight of glory;* **While we look not at the things which are seen, but at the things which are not seen: for the things which are seen are temporal; but the things which are not seen are eternal.**

During the health challenges, I never enjoyed the journey itself, but I did enjoy my relationship with God. I never once felt what many would say—"sick." It became an opportunity to get even closer to God, learning more and more about Him, feasting on His Word. It became an even better opportunity to witness. I think of one of my church mothers who had gone on to be with the Lord. Our Mission Ministry would go visit to cheer her and she would always bring cheer to us. That became a healing measure for me, spreading God's Word no matter what was staring me in the face. Those negative moments turned into positive moments once I started telling somebody about Jesus. I come to realize truly that He was in control. There were times when at home I may not have had my Bible in my hand, but God brought His Word to my remembrance and that gave me strength and courage to embrace the ups and the downs, to endure so that I would be able to tell somebody about Jesus on my journey. I kept a prayer journal through it all and I remember at Bible class one Wednesday evening I gave testimony to the fact that on my journey then and even now I came to truly know God the Father, God the Son, and God the Holy Spirit. I stated to the class that evening, "Whether I live or die, I win!" Remember God chose us to choose Him as in **John 15:16** *Ye have not chosen me, but I have chosen you, and ordained you, that ye should go and bring forth fruit, and that your fruit should remain: that whatsoever ye shall ask of the Father in my name, he may give it you.*

I repeat **Job 14:1** *Man that is born of a woman is of few days, and full of trouble.* To me, this is saying from the first sin in the Garden of Eden we were doomed to death, but because of **I John 2:1-2** *My little children, these things write I unto you, that ye sin not. And if any man sin, we have an advocate with the Father, Jesus Christ the righteous: And he is the propitiation for our sins: and not for ours only, but also for the sins of the whole world.* **John 3:16** *For God so loved the world, that he gave His only begotten Son, that whosoever believeth in Him should not perish, but have everlasting life.*

As I went through the ordeals of colon cancer and uterine cancer, back surgery, the threat of a bowel obstruction, and my husband's ordeal—in fact, throughout my whole life—I never walked alone. Those years of not knowing God, only *about* Him and, as I said previously, those were probably times that I didn't want to know Him, I never walked alone. We think what we don't know can't hurt us. How untrue! Just for a reminder: **Luke 12:47-48** *And that servant, which knew His Lord's will, and prepared not himself, neither did according to His will, shall be beaten with many stripes. But he that knew not, and did commit things worthy of stripes, shall be beaten with few stripes. For unto whomsoever much is given, of him shall be much required: and to whom men have committed much, of him they will ask the more.* What you don't know can hurt you.

Jesus, my Lord and Savior, was with me all the time. He confirmed to me that whether I lived in this world or I died, I won, as in **II Corinthians 5:8** *We are confident, I say, and willing rather to be absent from the body, and to be* **present with the Lord**. God had comforted me so, to come to realize the truth of that scripture, and therefore the spirit of fear did not touch me. My mind was sound. He gave me the power to trust and believe in Him by His Word. I don't know of anyone who truly wishes that they would die right here and now. In my years of nursing, I saw many who seemed to want to die because of pain and suffering. Years ago, one of my patients said, "Everybody wants to go to heaven, but nobody wants to die." Flesh and blood cannot inherit the Kingdom of Heaven (paraphrasing **I Corinthians 15:50a**). We have to die in the flesh in order to enter into Heaven in the *spirit*.

My sisters and brothers, there is a song called, "Only What You Do for Christ Will Last." He asks our obedience, as in **II Chronicles 7:14** *If my people, which are called by my name, shall humble themselves, and pray, and seek my face, and turn from their wicked ways; then will I hear from heaven, and will forgive their sin, and will heal their land.*

No matter what we may be going through, whether we think it to be bad or good, we are to trust and acknowledge God. **Proverbs 3:1-8** *My son, forget not my law; but let thine heart keep my commandments: For length of days, and long life, and peace, shall they add to thee. Let not mercy and truth forsake thee: bind them* *about thy neck; write them upon the table of thine heart: So shalt thou find favour and good understanding in the sight of God and man. Trust in the Lord with all thine heart; and lean not unto thine own understanding. In all thy ways acknowledge Him, and he shall direct thy paths. Be not wise in thine own eyes: fear the Lord, and depart from evil. It shall be health to thy navel, and marrow to thy bones.*

Our walk should be in line with our talk. We say we trust in God. We say we are leaning and depending on Him always; yet with the slightest variation from "our" planning and we go into sighting mode (walking by sight) instead of "faithing" mode (walking by faith). The scripture instructs us that "in all of our ways" we are to acknowledge God and He will direct our paths. He knows our every need and has promised to supply them according to His riches in glory by Christ Jesus (**Philippians 4:19**). **II Peter 3:9** *The Lord is not slack concerning His promise, as some men count slackness; but is longsuffering to us-ward, not willing that any should perish, but that all should come to repentance.*

Our goal as one that is saved, one that has confessed the Lord Jesus with thy mouth, and believing in thine heart that God hath raised Him from the dead (paraphrasing **Romans 10:9**); our goal is to live eternally with Jesus in heaven in "that world" for "this world is not our home." We are in the world; but not of the world (**John 17:14** *I have given them thy word; and the world hath hated them, because they are not of the world, even as I am not of the world*).

When everything in your life seems more than you can bear, when problems confront you, and there's no one to share, when there are mountains you cannot get through, remember, Jesus, He cares for you. The storm is passing over, the storm is passing over, the storm is passing over, Hallelujah!

The Storm is Passing Over

© John Eberhart, words and music; Wilma L. McGee, soloist.

Music Registration Number/Date: SRu000187143/1990-05-07

www.ingramcontent.com/pod-product-compliance
Lightning Source LLC
Chambersburg PA
CBHW052029290426
44112CB00014B/2445